Stars at Noon

Books by Enid Shomer

Poetry
Stars at Noon: Poems from the Life of Jacqueline Cochran (2001)
Black Drum (1997)
This Close to the Earth (1992)
Stalking the Florida Panther (1988)

Fiction
Imaginary Men (1993)

Stars at Noon

Poems from the Life of Jacqueline Cochran

by Enid Shomer

The University of Arkansas Press
Fayetteville
2001

05 04 03 02 01   5 4 3 2 1

Designer: John Coghlan

⊗ The paper used in this publication meets the minimum requirements
of the American National Standard for Permanence of Paper for Printed
Library Materials Z39.48-1984.

Library of Congress Cataloging-in-Publication Data

Shomer, Enid.
    Stars at noon : poems from the life of Jacqueline Cochran / by Enid
Shomer.
        p. cm.
      ISBN 1-55728-712-0 (alk. paper)
     1. Cochran, Jacqueline—Poetry. 2. Women air pilots—Poetry. 3.
Businesswomen—Poetry. I. Title.
      PS3569.H5783 S7 2001
      811'.54—dc21
                                                          2001002000

For Michael Neuwirth, M.D.,
master surgeon and mensch

Acknowledgments

I am grateful to the National Endowment for the Arts for two Fellowships in Poetry, and to the State of Florida for three individual artist's grants during the writing of this book. The Virginia Center for the Creative Arts has often been my writing home away from home, and some of these poems were written there. My thanks, also, to the librarians and archivists at the Dwight D. Eisenhower Presidential Library, especially Thomas Branigar, and to the editors of the following magazines and anthologies who first published these poems:

Apalachee Quarterly*: "Peace Comes to Tinian Island," "The Tiger of Malaya," "*Hakko Ichiu:* All Eight Corners of the World under One Roof," "Driving up Fangdou Shan Mountain," "The Ornament," "Yellow Air, Trees," and "After Visiting Hitler's Bunker"
Beyond Lament: Poets of the World Bearing Witness to the Holocaust (Evanston, Illinois: Northwestern University Press, 1998): "After Visiting Hitler's Bunker"
Cincinnati Poetry Review**: "Note Found with Infant in Mrs. Pittman's Bureau Drawer," "Letter from Anna Thompson to Mr. and Mrs. Pittman," "From Miss Bostwick to Her Family in Cincinnati," "Another Letter from Miss Bostwick to Her Family," "To Practice My Penmanship and Spelling," "In the Richler Household I Am the Shabbos Goy," "My Fancy Lady," "Laying out Papa," "First Flight," "Lighting Candles for Amelia," "On the Hustings with Rin Tin Tin," "An Interview with the Candidate," and "In the Desert"
International Quarterly: "Luna"
Louisville Review: "From the Rooftop of the Savoy Hotel"
Maryland Poetry Review: "Memo from a Speechwriter," "Darling, Some Last Minute Warnings," "To Fred Eldridge, after Defeating Him in the Republican Primary," and "Regarding Republican Solidarity"
Poet Lore: "The Mirror Divides" and "Kaffeeklatsch in Chungking"

*Under the title "Datelines: Jacqueline Cochran at War's End," these poems received the *Apalachee Quarterly* Long Poem Prize, sponsored by the National Endowment for the Arts.

**Ten of these poems were published as "Flights: Poems from the Life of Jacqueline Cochran," and received the *Cincinnati Poetry Review*'s award for best poem sequence.

Finally, I want to thank David Baker, Stacey Luftig, Alice Shields, Levent Tuncer, and Bibi Wein—friends and colleagues all.

Contents

AT FULL THROTTLE

ON THE HUSTINGS

GROUND TIME

Sawdust Road

Jacqueline Cochran (1906?–1980) is remembered as an aviator and as founder and director of the Women's Airforce Service Pilots (WASP) during World War II. An autodidact with only three years of formal education, Cochran held more speed, distance, and altitude records in her lifetime than any pilot of either sex and was the first woman in the world to fly faster than the speed of sound, as well as the first to attain Mach 2. At this writing, nearly forty years after she established them, five of her world speed records for reciprocating and turbo-jet aircraft still stand. From 1935 to 1963 she owned, operated, and personally promoted Jacqueline Cochran Cosmetics, headquartered in New York City, a signature line of expensive beauty products sold in department stores.

Outspoken and ambitious, Cochran remained active in aviation until she was sixty, ran for Congress, and generally placed herself in the path of history in a life she described as a "passage from sawdust to stardust." She was a devout Catholic.

Cochran began life as Bessie Mae Pittman, a foundling raised in crushing poverty on "Sawdust Road"—the company sawmill towns of the Florida Panhandle. At age six, she overheard her foster mother, whom she described as "slovenly, lazy, and mean," discussing the secret of her birth. The revelation that she was not related to her shiftless family relieved and exhilarated her. She left home at twelve, supporting herself as a midwife, maid, textile weaver, nurse, and beautician.

Muscogee, Florida, c. 1906

Note Found with Infant in Mrs. Pittman's Bureau Drawer

I'm fifteen and got no one.

I seen you many times
with your girls
at the company store
and Mr. Pittman
teamed with the ox on Sundays.

I don't know which
of the three boys to blame.
They said they only wanted
to touch me down there.
After, I prayed to the Virgin
for my monthlies
and confessed to the priest.

She's a good baby.
The night she came I dreamed
she climbed clear to heaven
like Jacob's angels.
So I named her Jacqueline.

All I can give her
is my mojo lamp, twelve
chips and this dollar.
Please send her to Mass each month
when the priest comes round.

Say I was French
not Cajun.

Letter from Anna Thompson to Mr. and Mrs. Pittman

Perhaps you've already heard
of Bessie Mae's vicious attack.
She beat me about the wrists
with my own ruler. I'm used
to the roughness of Sawdust Road,
but respect must be learned
before the ABCs.
This being only the third day
of school, I didn't stop her
when she bolted.

The children say she steals
chickens, luring them
with a kernel of corn
attached to a string.
She calls this "fishing."
She's been seen
with that foolish old Negro,
Aunt Jennie Smart.
Grandpa Whiskers fills her head
with lies like the ones
that provoked me today:
Bessie Mae lifted her dress
and pointing to her navel
claimed an Indian arrow
had made it. She said
after that she sat down
on an axe and that's why
she's only a girl.

You will please initial
this note and give it back
to the boy who brought it.

Bagdad, Florida, September 1913

From Miss Bostwick to Her Family in Cincinnati

Normal School did not prepare me
for this backwater.
Only one pupil is eager,
though completely unschooled.
I pay her ten cents a week
to haul firewood to my room.

She has a cherub's gold hair
but shucks oysters bare-
handed. On her first visit
I fed her stewed prunes.
She's never tasted an apple or pear
and wears flour sacks to school.
Her body is lithe
with outsized hands and feet.
But I must teach her to bathe!

Please send cured meat
as I tire of mullet and beans.
Each morning I wake to the gray-
bearded trees and think *they
are weary, like the people.*
I pray for you each night,
picture you swinging in the green
light of the willow. Despite
the distance between
us, I remain

   Your loving daughter

Bagdad, Florida, April 1914

Another Letter from Miss Bostwick to Her Family

I've settled into a pleasant routine.
Mornings, Bessie Mae comes
to fasten my corset and dress.
After school we chat and read.
She's begun *David Copperfield*
on her own, pausing only to ask
what new words mean.
She says she learned the ABCs
watching boxcars from her shack
by the swamp. It's true
she refused to go to school
all of last year.

She loves the dress and ribbon
I gave her and makes good use
of the comb. But "becoming a lady"
didn't stop her from climbing a tree
to peek into the Negro jook
across town. She dozed and fell
to the ground from her second-story
perch, luckily unhurt.

How I miss Ohio's orderly red
brick and honest cold.
Here, the children go without
shoes even in winter.
The company takes more
than virgin forests down
to stumps. A man lost
an arm this week in the band-saw
at the two-sided mill.

To Practice My Penmanship and Spelling

Mama just sits home.
The rest of us threw bricks
with the pickets at the cotton mill
and screamed *ten hour shifts!*
Better pay!

Still reading *Dracula.*
Today's words: *acumen,*
precipice, simoon.
Mama asked where did I read
before we had a bathroom.

A woman from the mill
told me to see the Richlers
who own three beauty shops in town.
She said I have "aims"
other children lack.

Tomorrow I'll cash in
the twelve Coke bottles
I found in the trash
for the nickelodeon show
at Skeeter Flats.

In the Richler Household I Am the Shabbos Goy

which means only I
light the fire, answer the phone
and cook on Saturdays.
I never bring *traif* to my room.

Mrs. Richler taught me
to "kosher the meat"—
to draw out the blood with salt
until it rinses clean

as the Monday wash. They think
eating blood can make you cruel.
But what of the Holy Communion
I take each week?

At the shop I mix
batches of henna and shampoo
but I'm learning to give
Nestlé permanent waves.

Columbus, Georgia, 1920

My Fancy Lady

She runs a "house"
for the men at the mill
but talks like a teacher
and dresses in silk.
She won't let me say "ain't"
and gave me *Jane Eyre*.

The stories she tells
of faraway cities
and fancy clothes
are so swell
I practically dye her hair
one strand at a time.

Today when I shampooed her
she grabbed my arm and said
Men promise anything
to get between your legs
but give you only
six inches of themselves.

Pensacola, Florida, 1923

The Death of Bessie Mae Pittman

It happened in the library
while I was browsing in the delicious
Britannica Cs—*caryatid,*
cataract, conch. My eye fell upon
COCHRANE, Thomas, Tenth Earl of Dundonald,
and I felt my foster family's name
slip away like a rock

down a well. "A British Admiral
with a long list of patents
to his credit." Lamps that burn
oil of tar. Schemes
for propulsion of ships at sea,
the rotary steam engine.

That night, I tuned my car
then practiced my new signature,
unfurling streamers from the Cs
like the ones in *Coca Cola.* My trademark
for a string of beauty shops:

**Jacqueline Cochran, Cosmetiste
Engine Valves Ground and Pincurls Set
with the Same Twist of the Wrist**

Flight

In 1932, the same year that she learned to fly, Cochran was sent by Antoine's of Saks Fifth Avenue to work the winter season as a hairdresser in the resorts of south Florida. There she met her husband, Floyd Odlum, self-made millionaire, head of the giant Atlas Corporation, and one of the wealthiest men in America. Theirs was a complex, loving union which lasted for forty years, until Floyd's death in 1976. They lived in New York City and Indio, California, where in the early thirties each bought acreage for date and citrus ranches which they later combined.

Cochran's passion in the air was for racing and record-setting. She quickly gained recognition as a daring, stylish, and unconventional pilot, second in fame only to her friend, Amelia Earhart. Her reputation as a navigator was peerless.

In June of 1941, before the United States entered the Second World War, Cochran flew a Lend-Lease bomber to England at President Roosevelt's request to demonstrate American support for Britain. She remained during the Blitz, organizing and training American women pilots for Britain's Air Transport Auxiliary (ATA). In 1943, she was appointed Director of the U.S. Women's Airforce Service Pilots (WASP). This corps of a thousand women ferried planes, towed targets, and performed other non-combat tasks to release male pilots for combat during the war. Despite Cochran's attempts in Congress to gain militarization for them, the WASPs were disbanded in 1945.

Miami Beach, 1932

Floyd

All day the surf
lathers the jetties while I pack
myself in sand,
like slipping under his freckled skin.
Did he notice
I stared at him through a five-course
meal? Later,
at the gaming tables, my fingers
crept over the felt.
I played blackjack but couldn't do math
and lost the hundred
he staked me to. O Father in Heaven!
I kept brushing
against him, I couldn't help myself.
I wanted to soften
the blades of his shoulders, to trace the line
from breastbone to navel,
that seam of hair fine as a baby's.
Twelve hours
since he walked me to my car,
and I still feel
his palm heating the small of my back.
This body refuses
to face facts: I'm a beautician
to this court,
a spunky kid without a home.
Floyd's forty,
Floyd's a millionaire, Floyd's
married, with two

young boys. Floyd, Floyd,
Floyd! I rub in
a little oil for you. I pretend
the sun has hands.

Laying out Papa

No embalming. No
ceremony. Just soap
and water, his skin
fragile as newsprint
that's been rained on and dried.

I bought a cheap pine
coffin without lining
or pillow—*we stay in the earth
so long*—laid his body
on the board table and began

to wash. Read his life
in scars: bayou, bandsaw,
Chip Charley, a woman
to get children on,
then dust.

I wasn't afraid to wash him
good. Afterwards,
my face floated in the dirty
basin, the mouth twisted,
asking *is this my life?*

Roosevelt Field, New York, 1932

First Flight

I thought I was flying
in my roadster until today.
This beats everything else
all to hell.

I don't understand
how the plane overcomes
gravity, but I do know
the force of will

that built it, the feel
of an open throttle in my hand,
the world passing beneath me,
silent and neat

as pages in a stamp album.
Thank God I've always lived by my hands,
for landing is all touch:
you put the nose down

and get up the speed
until the wires start to sing.
Then you pull the nose up
just enough to stop

the singing. Touching down, I could swear
I felt the tarmac
in my palms.
This is where I want to be—

between places, bound
only by a destination
that I reckon
by rivers and stars.

Indio, California, 1935

Photograph with Amelia

Here we are together in man-tailored clothes,
lace-up shoes, wind-raked hair. It's true:
to fly like a man, you must dress like one, pose

your limbs loosely, take up more room than a rose
on a thorny stem, shoulder your way into view.
Here we are together in man-tailored clothes

sitting on my diving board, two birds who chose
a lofty perch from which to pierce the blue.
To fly like a man, you must dress like one, pose

for the cameras, practice your braggadocios,
be interviewed up to the elbows in grease with the crew.
Here we are together in man-tailored clothes

sitting close as sisters. Below us, our shadows
on the water waver and merge into a new
woman who'll fly with men, dressed in the clothes

she wants. Amelia, let's be loud as crows!
And when we're miles apart, use ESP to see.
We're here together in our man-tailored clothes.
To fly, we've dressed like men. It's just a pose.

HOME FACIAL MANIPULATION
A Performance Poem For the Two Voices in Every Woman

HOW A WOMAN AGES

a woman ages from the neck up   as if struggling out of a noose
Not even spiral croquignoles   with silky loops, the last cry in
French permanent waves, can offset   her little mouth
cracks where lipstick bleeds and feathers like a ragged wing.

A HELPFUL TIP

The second and third fingers
are the cosmetic fingers,
Aviatrix explains, breathing
canned oxygen through a mask.
Inborn utensils for home facial
manipulation's three easy steps:

1. PET YOUR THROAT

Try hand-over-hand   To struggle free of the noose
upward strokes   imagine a heavy rope
apply the cream   whipping across your throat
continue rubbing briskly   forcing the skin ear-ward
until the whole area   gullet to breastbone
flushes pink   puddling with blood.

Read or perform this poem as follows: Read each pair of poems separately, from left to right, stopping at the line breaks. Then read them together, leaping the gap in the middle of the page. Thus, each pair makes three poems. The only exception is "A Helpful Tip."

2. IRON YOUR JAW

At the point of the chin
pressing your fingers
in a bracing rhythm
"iron" the bone
until your jaw tingles

Picture a rotary engine
humming your name
circle the world
until your ears
until all of you fills with applause.

3. LOVE YOUR CHEEKS

Press palms to face
flat as plates
Rotate until the cheeks glow

Even if you're scared they'll stack you
flat as paper dolls
Polish the brass in your knuckles.

REMEMBER THIS

Filles D'Eve
carry a flacon of cologne
dab a hint on your cheeks.
Massage your face every day
Only sleep removes fatigue
the sun has etched your face

Daughters of Eve
bring out the apple
The way you
read a compass—by degrees—
Little lines like crows' feet indicate places
as precisely as a clock marks time.

Los Angeles, July 5, 1937

Lighting Candles for Amelia

When you didn't arrive at Howland
I told GP what I "saw"—
the plane ditched,
Fred Noonan's skull split
against the bulkhead,
and you, adrift but alive
in the trackless Pacific.
I said *Itasca, a ship*
before I ever heard that name.

The searchers didn't know
we'd practiced ESP,
that you believed
I had the power to find you
if you ever went down.
For two days I watched you
pitch in feverish sleep
while the equatorial sun hung
like a mother's face at a sickbed.

Lighting these candles
I see your Electra glinting
as it tips into the sea.
If they ask me I'll say
your last flight was endless.
The body is only the plane,
Amelia, in which the soul rides.

Before winning the Bendix Transcontinental Air Race,
September 1938. Burbank, California, to Bendix, New
Jersey, in ten hours, seven minutes, and ten seconds.

My Lucky Thirteen

Unlucky, because the Last Supper fed
thirteen. *Very unlucky,* because it exceeds
by one the hinge pin of the Hebrew cosmos.
(Father Hailey claims that that's the source
of "cheaper by the dozen," that their heaven
consists of nothing but the number twelve!)
I believe in science, don't need the vaunted "7"
to keep my rotors spinning. With this "13"
I paint today on my fuselage, I praise
the Wright brothers, Seversky, Howard Hughes.
I offer a target, an invitation, a dare:
    Superstition, show your power, work
    your sour math, exhaust the very air!

London, 1942

From the Rooftop of the Savoy Hotel

How the city blackens when the air raid
siren wails! Whole blocks,
their windows draped or felted,
dim out like doused coals. You hear
planes grinding the air, then
silence, then—if you're close enough—
the sliding whistle of falling bombs.
Tonight, three dogfights overhead,
the East End a vast lake of flames.

When the knives of searchlights ply the sky
and the *ack-ack* guns bark from Hyde
Park, I can almost convince myself
it's a puppet show—Stukas and Spitfires
worked on wires, balloons tethered
to toy buildings with butcher's twine,
and behind a black scrim, their faces
ghoulishly lit from below, two
small boys screaming sound effects.

This rooftop is safer than any house—
no glass to shatter, no pipes exploding
to shrapnel, just this parapet
like a waist-high revetment.
Nothing to fall on my head,
though when they manage to pierce
the haze, the stars flare
like lit incendiaries.

Tomorrow at first light, people
will salvage singed photos, splintered
bedsteads, everything ruined reborn
as touchstone. For now, in pubs and homes,
beneath the streets in tube stations,
the Brits are carrying on, growing
closer. Yes. Imagine how easily
love would bloom in the last dark
room of your life.

Washington, D.C., 1943

The Generals Choose a Uniform

The wool I pulled over the generals' eyes
was a fine, Santiago-blue serge,
an A-line skirt and belted jacket
tailored at Bergdorf's to my design.

That's what the professional model wore.
I also paraded two dumpy Pentagon
typists, one in the Nurses' Corps
uniform (fashioned, I'd say, by Army snafu),

the other swathed in the green surplus
WAC fabric they've been waving at me
like a flag. George Marshall, ignoring all three,
picked the gray Chanel I had on,

bought in France before the War!
I commended him on his taste,
but didn't he think a uniform needed
pockets, flaps, and a little brass?

Blank stare. I swished my skirt
across his silence and quoted the price
I'd paid. "Ah money," he mused,
lurching forward like a cash drawer

without the bells, agreeing with Hap
on "the tall blue number."

Camp Davis, North Carolina, September 1943, after the
death of two WASPs. Sabotage was suspected.

Sugar Elegy

A silver spoon,
a thin white stream
like a contrail
tipped into my coffee,
the spoon thickening
to a fuselage, flying
lazy eights and chandelles
over the gunnery range.
Sugar sleeting the Outer Banks,
her Douglas Dauntless buried in it,
everything it covers mounded
like a grave. *Betty Taylor Wood*
Rest in—How many spoonfuls to make
an engine fail? Sweet sludge I found
in the gas tank. Maybe
half a cup. One
of the men? *We won't*
serve with powder puff
pilots. Have to
keep it quiet, sweet
Jesus, two of my squadron
dead in the first month.
My report coated with the same sticky
grit. Riffle the pages.
Any sound to smother the silence
each time I hear
her engine stall.

Datelines

Restless after the defeat of the proposal to militarize the WASP, Cochran devised a plan to witness firsthand the end of the war in the Pacific. The weekly magazine Liberty, *recently acquired by her husband, Floyd, hired her as a journalist—a job, she admitted, that was largely "a fake." On August 9, 1945, the day the atomic bomb was dropped on Nagasaki, Cochran embarked on a four-month tour through recent theaters of war that took her around the world—from the island bases of the Pacific, to the Philippines, Japan, China, and finally home via Europe. Her status as Special Consultant to the Army Air Forces, arranged by General H. H. "Hap" Arnold, gave her access to people and places off-limits to correspondents. Because she was not limited to covering hard news, she posted her bylined stories for* Liberty *wherever and whenever something piqued her interest.*

The Mariana Islands, at the Superfortress air base of the 58th Bombardment Wing, August 1945

Peace Comes to Tinian Island

The B-29s of Tinian
wear painted battle ribbons—
a bomb for every mission flown,
a rising sun for every Zero downed.
A trek over the hump
of the Himalayas earned a camel
loping along the silver
dune of the nose.
On the airstrip at noon
their great metal hulks
blaze like suns.
But airborne, it was night
they carried in their bays,
death they draped
over New Guinea, the Bismarck Sea.

When they flew in low today,
unannounced, during the exhibition
baseball game, the pitcher's
arms went limp,
the catcher came uncaged
and all talk stopped.
Huge shadows roared across
my face, sorting through
the bleachers the way I imagine
God checked the doorposts
in Egypt for blood.

When they had gone
there was hot tropical
light again, our own voices
cheering the runner home.

The Tiger of Malaya

Scoured from the jungle,
General Yamashita paces
near our convoy

on the asphalt runway,
considering his fate.
He requests a Chesterfield

and lights up slowly,
white plumes
streaming from his nose,

unraveling in the air
like twin ropes.
They say a noose

will soon yank him home
to his ancestors,
that the old samurai,

bereft of their masters,
retired to monasteries
to write poetry,

or committed *seppuku*
believing death, like art,
was a form of perfection.

New York City, 1945

The Mirror Divides

Dearest Jackie,

Each morning over coffee
I finger the globe
like a huge worry bead
to keep you safe in Guam,
Okinawa, China, Japan.
I comb the *Times,* forbidding
your name to appear.
Ditto the radio,
whose static always sounds
like a preface to doom.

Last night, I wore
your favorite dinner jacket,
the cook prepared oysters
in the shell, and yellow roses
lit the table.
If I can't have you with me,
I want every room filled
with your absence,
each door leaning open
on an aching hinge.

Now your expressions
surface in my speech,
your gestures in my body!
I remember as a small boy
on days my father paid

pastoral calls to the sick,
I'd wear his wingtips,
clunking through the house
to conjure his safe return.

I walked into your closet tonight:
shoes paired like colorful mating
birds, silk dresses still
as a long intake of breath,
your smell, and myself repeated
in the full-length panel mirrors.
Darling, we are divided now
only as the mirror divides
an object into two—
through illusion.

My darling, wherever you go
in the Pacific, take along
this white wish, this slip
of sympathetic magic.
Tuck it inside
your regulation shirt—
the left-hand pocket—
so my uphill cursive
can leap in praise
against your heart.

Oceans of love,

Floyd

Near Hachioji, Japan

Hakko Ichiu: All Eight Corners of the World under One Roof

A wall of weather
around Hiroshima again—
not even a glimpse
of the moon-pocked terrain
through that heavy scrim—
so we flew back to Atsugi
and jeeped to Tokyo. Forty miles
of refugees living in paper
or tin lean-tos, the stench
of night soil in honey buckets.
The brass claims the A-bomb saved
lives when it gathered two cities
into towers of smoke
20,000 feet high.

All along the roads,
families huddle around
their household safes
which once hid the makings
for magnetos and propeller hubs.
Most of them are open now,
the tumblers removed.
Instead of machine tools,
the safes hold infants
who pedal the air
as if to work free
of their heavy steel cribs.
How perfectly the cornerless sky
fits their dainty feet.

Driving up Fangdou Shan Mountain

Yesterday, pigtail flying,
his clothes a useless sail,
a coolie fell from a rooftop

and was left to whimper
in the street, the passersby
struck deaf and blind

by the custom that decrees
if you save a Chinaman,
you must support his family

for life. *Protocol!* my military
aide shouted, stopping me
when I rose to help.

Later, on the road to Chungking,
the ascent too steep
for our carcass of a jeep

jerry-rigged with chicken-wire,
I saw him plunge at each
precipice, inconsequential

as the spit of stones
thrown up by our wheels.
At last we reached a level plain

with groves of tung oil trees,
their brown drupes clattering
in the wind like small wooden

temple bells. He fell to earth
as if a cloud had cast him down,
part storm, part shadow.

Tachikawa, Japan, 1945

Feminine Protocol

Dear Jackie:

Enclosed is the certificate
you wanted to make it official:
you were the first American
woman to occupy Japan after V-J Day.
(Gen. Kreuger's forces
secured Kyoto—two days late—
only hours after we left!)

We should have drawn hazard pay—
landing a bucket C-47
on wet turf, then leaving it
with that rheumy-eyed Papa-san
sitting on the airfield
in his rocking chair.
And you, running through town,
tapping on windows in a war zone
to bring the locals out!

Have you deciphered the prayer
the temple priest scratched
for us on parchment? My guess
is that it says *may you go far
away, where you came from.*

Jackie, I'll never forget how
you explained to that old Jap gent
in the Edwardian get-up

that you and I were an advance guard,
then slipped off your shoes
and occupied a department store
to buy silk at bargain prices.

Safe passage home to USA-jima.

Cordially,

Anky
Maj. Gen. Francis Leroy Ankenbrandt

Chungking

The Ornament

The clocks in China might as well
be turned to the wall for all
the respect paid to time.
I was soaking in the bath, warm
braziers at either side, laying down
a ring of road filth wide
as a tire tread, when a servant knocked
(way before 1:00, the appointed hour)
and said, "Madame will see you. *Now.*"
I trekked through a drizzle
to the main complex, my uniform
wilting, anger my only rouge.

Her house looked airlifted
from Connecticut—clapboard siding,
colonial settees, at every window
priscillas swagged to ruffled smiles.
But a green fire smoldering
on the mantle caught my eye,
a huge Ming jade, enormous
jewel where light plunged and died,
bottomless as the Florida springs
where I swam as a girl.
A whole lifetime, Madame Chiang
explained, and part of two others

had been spent taming this rock.
My hands ached at the intricate
carved scene of tea in a pagoda garden—

minute blossoms and cups, a scuffed
gravel path. The workmanship
was perfect, as if light itself had etched
the folds of silk robes into the crevices,
the way canyons are sculpted by water
and grit. I thumbed the ebony
base. To be born and seated
in front of a small boulder.
Hands trained around hammer and chisel

would grow gnarled, twisted
to the one task: to free the tiny
figures trapped in the rock,
to give birth through a stone tunnel.
Madame was unmoved when my eyes
filled with tears. I wanted to say
I preferred Woolworth's celluloid jade
with its mold seams and blurred faces
to this masterpiece whose oily luster
reflects the slow subtraction of lives,
to this clock whose only hands
are human ones chipping away at time.

Near Wuchang, China, 1945

Yellow Air, Trees

Yellow air, trees
swaying on their pedestals,
a skein of women unwinding
through a field, bearing ramie
to be woven into coarse cloth.

Today, behind the wheel,
I entered at last the serene
China of landscape painting,
of silk scrolled around
the ancient pieties.

When swarms of children dart
in front of the jeep, my aide
shouts *DRIVE AS THOUGH
THEY AREN'T THERE.* They believe
if their shadow is crossed by a car

or plane, the devil will be cut
from their lives. My nerves fire
as each one dances across
the moving blade we make.
I understand the confusion

between machine and God,
between the powerful
and the Unseen. Before each race
I always remind myself
it is not the plane that keeps me up

but the thin air.

Kaffeklatsch in Chungking

Madame Chiang Kai-shek
is a graduate of Wellesley,
fluent in English and French,
yet I couldn't budge her
past kitchen chitchat—

cuisine and dress.
For two hours she compared
fabrics East and West,
explained the subtle fashion
changes year to year

in traditional Chinese garb—
the depth of notch in the Mandarin
collar, the direction in which
braid coils into toggles and frogs.
In the middle of our meal

she prepared soup at the table,
her hands describing flourishes
above the steam as she confided
to me the culinary code
of China: since soup fills

the belly fast, if the poor
serve it first, they're trying
their best to satisfy.
Served first by the rich,
it's a bowl of insult.

Later, she pinned me with silver
Chinese Air Force wings.
When I reached to shake her hand,
she twittered and blushed,
then covered her mouth

with a scarf withdrawn
from her sleeve, hidden there
all day, a wisp of silk
with the weight of stone.

After Visiting Hitler's Bunker

They say he was crazy,
that all of Germany warped
to his will. Having seen
the pictures from Dachau, Belsen,
having seen his bunker,
I tell you this:
Hell is equipped
with air conditioners.
A library. Rooms lined with cots
where children are permitted to dream
before they are poisoned. Evil
blooms not in chaos,
but order—in a train schedule,
a shower head, a wall—
its roots in the human
brain, two lobes split
like the serpent's tongue.

At Full Throttle

In 1953, flying a jet rented from the Canadians because her own government refused her one, Cochran again achieved world-wide notice, this time by setting a new world speed record and being the first woman to break the sound barrier.

In the 1960s, determined to play a role in the jet phase of aviation, Cochran's principal interest continued to be flying. On June 6, 1960, she became the first woman in the world to fly at Mach 2, twice the speed of sound. Nine days later, she became the first woman to make an arrested landing in a jet on an aircraft carrier. On April 27, 1962, she was the first woman to pilot a jet aircraft across the Atlantic. In May of 1963, at age fifty-seven, Cochran set another new world speed record: 1,203.94 mph over a one-hundred-kilometer closed course, nearly twice the speed of her flight in 1953. Besides these landmark flights, she set numerous other altitude, speed, and distance records, all with an eye to becoming the first woman in space. She lobbied her powerful friends in government and the military to no avail: her age and deteriorating health were insuperable obstacles.

She sold her interest in Jacqueline Cochran Cosmetics in 1963.

After the fifth miscarriage

Luna

Except where its face is webbed
with a newborn's caul, the moon
afloat in my binoculars tonight
looks transparent as a cell
under a microscope.
Three weeks ago, a crescent
leaned in the sky like a woman
reveling in her bath, unbloodied
water dripping through her fingers
like soft stars.

In the near distance
tamarisk trees like lines of chalk,
the raked gravel path
swollen with light. All women
wish for this: to wax, then wane,
disappearing at last
into their children.

On my window sill, pebbles and pods
arranged like a worship,
small irregular moons offered
to the large and perfect one.
I think of the women before me
who translated birdsong
into birthmark and charted
her phases. So much science
and so much prayer and still she pulls
my sons from me.

Spring, 1952

To Mr. John Jay Hopkins of Canadair

Kind Sir:

I'm writing today to request the rental
of a jet—a new Orenda-powered
F-86. Before the Japs scoured
Pearl, I ferried the first Lend-Lease

bomber to England. (A man had to land us!
A woman, they said, at the stick "looked frivolous.")
Now again Washington ties my hands,
refuses me jets. If you grant me the privilege,

I hope to set the speed record, pluck
that flower from the air as I dive through
the sound barrier at Edwards, a desert of lake
beds and salt flats perfect for scraping

to a halt from fifty thousand feet. I'll foot
the $10,000 tab to insure the craft,
marshal support among the top brass,
keep in the dark all the Congressional boot-
lickers who never polished my pumps, and ask
my priest to look up when he celebrates morning Mass.

Yours with gratitude,

Jackie

The Remarkable Story of Jacqueline Cochran and the Wilted Corsage

She looked at limp gardenias
and saw not a rusting bouquet
but a great truth: the dewiness
of youth depends upon moisture.
Mother Nature is less ruthless
when drunk with essential oils.
If you can't keep blooms plumped
and erect except immersed in water,
why do women butter their faces
with heavy unguents and creams?

Months later, from her chemists' retorts
dripped pearls of *Hydrolin,*
the secret ingredient that waters
the skin, penetrates like rain
into thirsty soil. *Flowing Velvet.*
Available in fine stores.
Contains no hormones. Guaranteed
to leave no greasy stains.

Flight attaining Mach 1, Edwards Air Force Base,
California, June 1953

The World Goes Black

TAKE-OFF

How featureless the earth
as it recedes, each green
valley and hill devoid of curves

and definition, settling
into swirls of rubbed pastels,
the salt flats below me

ridged like a tidal sea
and the sea with its rolling feathers
suddenly still.

All around me, sky
streams past, long blue
corridor to the night. Huge clouds

stretch from horse heads
to a kind of history,
another world curled

in their roiling manes.

ASCENT

Today I thank God for my hands,
so big they attract stares

even manicured, nails short
as a general's patience.

Big fidgety anchors, Mama laughed,
Keep them in your lap!
They seem enlarged, the Army doctor
wrote, *by some crushing*

physical task. "Like shucking
oysters?" I saluted him
so they dwarfed my cap.
I've tried dark gloves so women

wouldn't notice. It made things
worse when I took them off.
In WASP dress white gloves,
clown hands waved.

They should see my feet.

DIVE FROM 45,000 FEET

Swathed in silence I drop,
the bones of my skull
thrumming against my brain.

Time is like an elastic band
the way it stretches and zings
back. My audience with the Holy Father—

four minutes, his chamberlain warned—
stretched into twenty-eight, passing
in one quick exhilarated gasp

while these forty-five seconds
slowed to cold molasses, time
enough to review a parade

of my life, catch destiny
waiting outside my cockpit
for one mistake, red-eyed

as the eject button. I fasten on
the machmeter, the needle
approaching and approaching,

like a body forging toward pleasure,
that point when I begin to beg
when nothing else matters

and the world goes black
as the world of the blind where touch
is everything, the only thing,
the thing next to holy.

The Heaven of Names

Mr. Dudley Cloud, Director
Atlantic Monthly Press
Boston, Massachusetts

My dear Dudley,

L'Air du Temps, Breathless Mist,
Fille D'Eve—fragrances,
like biography, distill
the essence. Now, thanks
to your patient editing, my life
is stoppered like perfume.

As you suggested, I played
with all the titles
until each nuance bloomed.
Aces, Queens and Generals
sounds like a busted straight!
And *Flights and Fancies* conjures up
crochet hooks and shawls.

You admit *Stars at Noon* is good
because of "the little paradox
it contains" (I had to look up
"paradox!"), but worry that readers
will be confused. Let them learn
that day is a kind of heavy

ground fog, that while we hustle
and plan according to sunnier
logic, the stars stare down
in their black hoods,
steady as a Greek chorus,
our destiny and our doom.

Until now, I'd grabbed at words
like doorknobs. Thank you
for teaching me to savor them like wine.
"Thank you" is so lame!
I'm shipping a bushel of dates
from my ranch, sweet
syllables in any tongue.

One hundred and four young women in white gowns, sponsored by Jacqueline Cochran Cosmetics at a cost of $10,000, were presented to society. Waldorf-Astoria Hotel, New York City, 1955

At the Debutantes' Cotillion

What would I give to wear
a feedsack shift again
and stand barefoot
in the restless silk of the stream,
the smell of the mill thick
on the air as fire, the saws
singing like sour violins?

What would I give to be eight
in a shoe store buying high heels
and see my reflection whole
for the first time, not broken
as the moon is over the swamp,
not a face like a dirty saucer
in Mama's crazed compact?

What would I give to see Myrtle
stirring indigo in a vat,
to dip my dress in,
then scraps of quilt and finally
my hands, my fingers
branching into the blue
like treetops into the sky?

What would I give to see the first fish
I caught and cleaned

flashing its silver
like a split roll of coins,
its guts floating away like beautiful
beads, all that slippery
life on my hands.

On the Hustings

In 1956, Cochran ran as a Republican for the U.S. House from the 29th Congressional District in California, where she and Floyd owned a six-hundred-acre citrus and date ranch. Her chances were excellent: her flying skill and her war work had earned the public's admiration. Her autobiography, written without the aid of a collaborator and published in 1954, had been widely reviewed and read.

Her serious competition in the primary was Fred Eldridge, author of Wrath in Burma, *a firsthand account of failures in Allied cooperation during World War II. Eldridge was also well-known as a past member of the United World Federalists (UWF), a respectable one-world government movement. The struggle between Cochran and Eldridge deteriorated into vicious personal attacks.*

Her Democratic opponent in the general election was Dalip Singh Saund, a native of India. The rhetoric of all the candidates was marked by the polarization and paranoia that characterized the McCarthy era. Cochran waged a tireless campaign, logging more than thirty thousand air miles in the primary alone, and was considered the favorite.

Indio, California, 1956

Memo from a Speechwriter

For the tenth time: patronage
from Hearst is the kiss
of death, especially those photos
of you sunning by your pool.
The little woman in Riverside
who slugs all day at a drill press
resents your strapless tan.
We've got six months to turn around
your Wealthy Dame P.R. Your rich
friends will still support you: they understand
a politician, like a bridge,
sways a little to span the gap.

Go help a guy dig a ditch,
jack up the car for Suzy Blow's flat,
even if you have to arrange it.
Democratic hearts defrost fast
in someone else's sweat.
Canvass your district in your plane
if you must, but land at a farm
and ride in on a truckload
of melons. In impromptu remarks,
pat the unionist on the back
for the honest dirt under his nails.
Attack public utilities.

To the veteran, preach defense.
Don't hint that Reds are seeping

into government, just say
every stinking Commie should be
shot.
      Attached is a statement
I doped out today, your stand
on industry for Coachella
Valley. READ FROM IT at the rally.
In politics, we don't fly
by the seat of our pants, we don't rely
on memory, and guts are what
we throw away of fish.

An Interview with the Candidate

Q: Now that you've tossed your
   Lily Daché bonnet in
   the ring, is it true

   you'd chemically
   seed the clouds to fight drought in
   Imperial County?

A: Rainmaking

   The cumulus clouds
   pack up their satchels of rain—
   drifters skipping out

   on rent. I believe
   with the Indians that wild
   horses graze a great

   plains in the sky, fed
   on bales of fog, restrained by
   lightning's brief corrals.

   Rain falls not when they
   stampede, but when they sleep, each
   drop a ripe pasture

   in dreams. The Upper
   Colorado is parched. Let's
   harness the dreaming

sky horses in that
Basin, bridle them with bits
of silver dropped from

planes.

Darling, Some Last Minute Warnings

Jackie—

Expect surprises in the last
days before the primary,
rumors injected
under the collective skin,
bogus facts slung like stones
against your religion, wealth,
residence in the East, your sex.
(O here I must digress:
every inch of you gets my vote!)

They'll tuck you in bed
with big business, claim you farm
the canyons of Wall Street,
not the desert of Indio.
They'll drag in our friendship
(that word in quotes) before my divorce,
print photos of our golf course,
dub your Lodestar a flying throne.

Then most false, most false
insinuate that I have been the pilot
of your life everywhere but in a plane.
If only they knew how it really is:
I was made from *your* rib.

Floyd

To Fred Eldridge, after Defeating Him in the Primary

I'm sending back the crow you set loose
to cackle untruths: immoral visits to my home
by Catholic priests? The Holy See of Rome
plucking California citrus and grapes?
Let the black bird in, listen to my litany:
only a Red would dedicate his book "to the Chinese
soldier" and claim our GIs looted Germany
of everything from Lugers to polo ponies.

I doubt you are even a real Republican!
That skeleton in your closet, the UWF,
rattled louder each time you scoffed
at doubts of your loyalty. Damn your one-world, one-man
support! Oiled wings flap at your tent while you search
for the reasons you lost, shoulders hunched to a perch.

Jackie

Regarding Republican Solidarity

Jackie—

Consider this a love letter, the Dear
John sort. I won't endorse your campaign
now or ever. If I was a traitor to join
the UWF, was Albert Einstein, Walter
Reuther, Norman Cousins? Public office
isn't about fleecing votes from sheep
but listening for the wolf's soft step.
You travel at the speed of sound, the voice

of the people trailing behind like a sonic boom.
Now you strafe the Democrat, call him a "man
from the lusty Punjab" whose "dark Hindu blood
will cripple him in the congressional cloakroom."
Come November, I hope your hide is tanned,
your face made-up like a loser's—with egg and mud.

Fred Eldridge

On the Hustings with Rin Tin Tin

Like the quartered steers that turned
all day on spits, I slowly roasted
in shirtwaist dress and stockings
while 4,000 voters ate barbecue
despite the worst dust storm
of the year. How many pounds of grit
seasoned the slaw and beans
I can only guess.

At last, I spoke for fifteen minutes,
my tongue stiffened to emery board
by desert wind and nerves.
Water, water, I said, *blood
for the body of the land,* etc.,
exactly as rehearsed. The orchestra
struck up "Thanks for the Memory"
and Bob Hope appeared,

followed by Roberta Linn,
Roz Russell, Gene Austin,
the Trio Tropicana,
Guadalajara Boys, Ponce Sisters
of Cuba, maracas, cucarachas,
the works! By eight o'clock
a squeaky floorboard sounded
like music to me.

I'd been briefed on all the issues—
a fistful of notecards

growing yeasty in the heat.
But they scrubbed my stirring farewell
for the dog from the movies.
He took center stage, spoke, played
dead, scaled a wall, and retrieved
a glove, never lifting his leg.

Navigating the Airwaves

Q: How would you describe
   your personality? Should
   the voters trust you?

A: You can't beat around
   the bush, fence-straddle, or lie
   in Mach 1 nose dives.

Q: Can you summarize
   your experience in the
   cosmetics business?

A: Gristle of boar hog,
   purple of thistle, nectar
   of jasmine: lipstick.

Q: Wouldn't your career
   have fallen flat without your
   money and status?

A: Privilege pulls no
   strings in the cockpit. Wealth can't
   float you through thin air.

Q: In general, do
   you believe that women should
   enter politics?

A: A woman's soft skin
   and pink cheeks don't mean she's weak,
   hot, or full of shame.

*At the ranch in Indio after the final tally revealed that Cochran had
lost by a scant 3,000 votes. November 7, 1956*

In the Desert

There is a woman
in the moon tonight, hazy
as the last breath
I once saw fogging a mirror
when a mill worker died.
She dips her toothless jaw
into a thin gruel of clouds
and is not nourished. . . .

God rested here in the desert
after Creation. He wanted
to empty himself of all
those designs for fin,
thorn, and claw. He was sick
of the gap-toothed smile
of mountains, the insistent wishing
of streams.

Whenever I find the skull
of an animal, I tell myself
it's a bead He rubbed
Himself to sleep with.

I want to empty myself like that.
I want to fall all the way
to ordinary.

Ground Time

Jacqueline Cochran continued to fly for pleasure, to support the Campfire Girls and other causes dear to her, and to collect the honors bestowed on her. But she spent much of the last two decades of her life in private, at home with Floyd, whose rheumatoid arthritis, first diagnosed in the 1940s, continued to worsen. She enlarged the facilities of the ranch in Indio, including an office addition so that President Eisenhower could work there for weeks or months at a time when he visited Palm Springs. Other dignitaries and celebrities also enjoyed the ranch on a regular basis. Jackie was a popular public speaker during these years, often lecturing on the peaceful uses of atomic energy.

In addition to her many flying medals and trophies, she received the U.S. Distinguished Service Medal for her war work; the French Legion of Honor; honorary wings of the French, Chinese, Turkish, Spanish, and Royal Thailand air forces; as well as honorary degrees from colleges and universities, including the Harvard Business School.

She died in 1980.

Pacemaker

Polished and gleaming alloys,
     greased gears,
the blue exhaust of a prop,
     white trail of a jet,
sound of a piston pumping,
     metallic sweat

of engine bushings, garrulous
     chatter of wheels on runways.
For years I prepared myself
     for the horizon to tilt
like a tray while I rode
     the latest machine built

to rise without wings,
     faster than sound, eight
"Gs" pressing me flat
     as a sheet. *NASA Names*
Cochran First Female
     Astronaut . . . A Dame

in Space! Symington tried.
     LBJ. *Too old,*
the Air Force said. Did they mean
     too much breast and thigh?
Too much trouble
     to pee inside a flight-

suit? Body more like a flower
     than a nail shooting through
earth's gravitational
     shell to the Vast,

where theorems predict celestial
       orbits lapse

into ellipses, and matter
       behaves strictly according
to math, as if numbers led
       a life excluding chance,
singular as the pin
       where Augustine's angels danced.

But metal fatigues like flesh,
       tires like a heart
that needs a jolt to keep
       its rhythm right. The machine's
inside me now,
       current jumping a gap.

1975

On the Road to Abilene

1.

Driving east from Colorado
across the held breath
of the high plains
you can still see the ruts
of the Conestogas,
feel the dust tighten
like sutures on the skin.
Imagine it: months thin as the ribs
of the canvas bonnet.
Hardtack, soda bread.
Then the sod house, that odor
of fresh grief. Nights,
the stars wheeled past,
saying *distance, time.*
Days, the horizon lay
like a knife upon a shelf.
What could I have made
of such limitlessness?
Of the herds that graze
as if lost, of the pious sway
of wheat? *Prairie fever* they call it,
though there was no heat last year
with Floyd's son, his head
so full of nothingness
only a gun could empty it.

2.

Who will finger the satin
tassels of my menus from Shanghai,
the design Franco himself sketched
for my gold airplane brooch (one ruby,
forty brilliants, in the propeller hub)?

Who will read the love
letters from Floyd? My medical records?
From this treasure and dross they tell me
a scholar can re-weave a life. I picture
a beautiful stranger in a tailored suit

who'll wear lipstick and comb her hair
at coffee breaks, appreciate
my tatting as well as my flying skill.
But how will she know my thrill beating
General Spaatz at poker in the Philippines?

I vomited when Cecil Allen
took off before me in the Bendix of '35
and burned to char on a power line.
Will she, merely reading my
account? Will she faint time and again

from the pain I suffered all my life
after the cheap appendectomy
I had at twenty? Will she look up
"noble plication"? Understand
the doctor stitched my adhesions shut

like a fan but couldn't unstick the tubal
scars that deprived me of daughters and sons?
Will she be pretty enough to know
how I felt when I hit fifty
and stopped caring about my looks?

(Or should I say my looks stopped
caring about me?) Maybe
I should leave a note, express
my reservations, clarify
the muddy stuff, explain why

I purged my files, claiming fire
and flood. Or maybe
I should not.

3.

Cremate me. I want
to leave them as I always
left them—looking up.

The Angel Floyd

Every formation of clouds
is a crowd of them whose God,
busy with punishment and reward,
has forgotten the soft gauze of their wings,
the weather they make when they're bored.

Through the night's dark glass
they dance against the *mise en scene*
of the moon or strum a beguine
in the orange trees whose flowers
smell the way angels must smell, preened

of all human failings though still human
in form, like the dead stars we see burning.
He came to me, legs and arms
muscled and whole, whose ankles
couldn't be touched, who winced

when shaking hands.
Wherever disease had deformed
the limbs shone with the gold
the doctors had injected. Gold tendons
rippled his loins. Floyd's skin always

smelled sweet as a baby's, even filmed
with sweat. All our married life
I breathed in this outward scent
of his goodness as I lay sighing
in our bed, also that pomade

he believed kept him from going gray.
At work, he went through people
like hot steel. But at home,
he couldn't fire the lazy gardener,
left all the dirty work for me.

Now, like stage lights pooling
behind him, his wings unfold.
As if shushing someone
to sleep, the trees rustle their branches.
He does not turn, but if he did,

what would he apprehend
with his celestial senses?
Not my voice, not my arms
flailing semaphores for love
and safe landing, but my grief

and with it, tears, and in them
flung light years from where
they began, the stars
of our Maker, shining.

Afterword by Her Biographer

AGAINST THE ODDS

I never knew her, never wanted to fly.
I found her, like so many truths, in a book—
a compendium of Floridians overlooked
and about to sink into anonymity
instead of sailing clear of the straits
of time. Her life helped me finally erase
statistics the freshman dean had placed like a curse
on my class: *Half of you will contemplate;*
half will act. Look to your right and left.
One in three girls will be mentally ill. I wanted
to ask if that counted toward the contemplative half
or meant no life at all for those haunted
by doubt. *One in ten, I regret to report,*
will be dead before she's begun—by the age of forty.

GIVING HER WORDS

I couldn't have given her *caryatid,*
braggadocio, and *simoon*
if all her life, poet-like,
she hadn't collected words, daily

jottings with *palimpsest, colloid,*
canticle, plinth. It's rare for a person
of action to settle into *Webster's* for a trip.
She never strung together the jewels

she culled from books. But she wanted
to spell them right if the occasion
ever arose. Most of all,
she needed to know what they meant.

HER VOICE

In Kansas, I listen to her voice recorded
fifty years ago

on red wax cylinders, only one
of which was transferred

to audio tape. (Without the defunct play-back
machine, the others are mute.)

Stored like honey in a hive, now her voice
flows again, deep

amber and smoky. A sergeant's bark for the times
when a voice soft as a skein

of wool would be ignored. At the end of each
remark something is crouched

waiting to pounce, as when the tympanist stands
over his cymbals and kettle

drums, loud crashes coiled in his wrists.
Ike and I were jeeping

from Berlin. . . . She savors the names of celebrities,
slows them on her tongue:

Frank-a-lin and Elay-ah-nor. . . . This voice
is conversant with battles, atomic

bombs, the strategies that reduce men
to pushpins on a map.

The voice cracks from booze and cigarettes
and grief; grief shatters

the words into jagged bits so the feeling bleeds
through, like daylight around

the frame of a weathered door. This is the voice
that announced a WASP was missing

over the Outer Banks, another riddled
with friendly fire over

the ordnance range. Sometimes the voice lifts me
as you'd lift someone who's wounded,

its drone rising and falling, like a life
raft on the open sea.

Sometimes the voice carries me past all
the wartime dying, as a mother

carries a sleeping child, not so much
to keep the child from waking

as to be there when she wakes.

Photographs

Frontispiece from Cochran's autobiography: a rosette of photographs of her in many guises, including elephant rider in the circus at Madison Square Garden.

Cochran in the 1930s.

Cochran and Amelia Earhart relaxing on the diving board at Cochran's ranch in Indio, California.

Cochran in her WASP uniform.

Cochran in 1963, about to pilot a jet at age fifty-seven.

Notes on the Poems

Note Found with Infant in Mrs. Pittman's Bureau Drawer

Workers on Sawdust Road were paid with company currency called "chips" (probably from "chits"), which they exchanged for virtually everything—provisions at the company store, rent, and medical care. The paymaster was usually called "Chip Charley."

As a young woman, Cochran asked her local priest to investigate the circumstances of her birth. He produced a sealed envelope containing information about her biological parents which Cochran kept in a lockbox unread until the end of her life, when she burned it.

Lighting Candles for Amelia

"GP" was the nickname of George Putnam, Amelia Earhart's husband.

Home Facial Manipulation

Much of the language for this poem is taken from ad agency campaign materials and actual advertisements in *Vogue* for Jacqueline Cochran Cosmetics.

After an air race, Cochran often powdered her nose and combed her hair in full view as she posed for photographers.

The Generals Choose a Uniform

"Hap" was the nickname of Gen. H. H. Arnold. The WASPs were the first fliers to wear the color later known as Air Force blue.

While they flew, the 1,074 women of the WASP were civil servants, without military standing, military pay scale, or veteran's benefits. They received retroactive military standing thirty-three years later, in 1977.

Hakko Ichiu: **All Eight Corners of the World Under One Roof**
Translated as "all eight corners of the world under one roof,"
Hakko Ichiu was the foreign policy doctrine which motivated
Japan's attempt to dominate the Pacific basin and her entry into
the War. It was based on traditional samurai values as well as Japan's
exposure to nineteenth-century European colonialism.

After Visiting Hitler's Bunker
Cochran bribed two Russian soldiers with ten dollars and a
pack of American cigarettes to gain entry into the heavily guarded,
looted, and gutted German headquarters. The cots in the poem
belonged to Goebbel's six children, all of whom were given
cyanide.

To Mr. John Jay Hopkins of Canadair
The F-86 is also known as the Sabre-jet. The world speed
record (over a one-hundred-kilometer closed course) was 635
mph. Cochran attained 652.5 mph.

The World Goes Black
Seven years later, on June 6, 1960, Cochran became the first
woman in the world to fly at Mach 2, twice the speed of sound.
In May 1963, at the age of fifty-seven, she set another new world
speed record: 1,203.94 mph over a one-hundred-kilometer closed
course, close to twice the speed of her flight in 1953.

An Interview with the Candidate
Cochran advocated seeding clouds with silver iodide to pro-
duce rainfall for drought-plagued Imperial Valley.

On the Road to Abilene
Cochran donated her papers and assorted memorabilia to the
Eisenhower Presidential Library in Abilene, Kansas.

The Angel Floyd

Floyd, who founded the Arthritis Foundation, suffered from crippling and excruciating rheumatoid arthritis. He underwent painful injections of gold salts in the forties and fifties.

About the Author

Enid Shomer is the author of three other books of poetry: *Stalking the Florida Panther* (The Word Works, 1988), winner of the Washington Prize; *This Close to the Earth* (Arkansas, 1992); and *Black Drum* (Arkansas, 1997). Her book of stories, *Imaginary Men* (Iowa, 1993), won the Iowa Fiction Prize and the LSU/*Southern Review* Prize, both given annually for the best first collection by an American author. Her poems and stories have appeared in *The New Yorker, Poetry, The Atlantic, Best American Poetry*, and many other magazines and anthologies. She has been visiting writer at the University of Arkansas, The Ohio State University, and Florida State University.